Here I am

Published in 2015 by
Daniel Murphy, Killeentierna, Currow, Killarney, Co. Kerry
email: dtmurphy@eircom.net

Photographs © Daniel Murphy

ISBN: 978-0-9931871-0-0

Book Design and typesetting by Anú Design, Tara
(www.anu-design.ie)

Printed by Dargan Press
(info@darganpress.co.uk)

Distributed by Gill & Macmillan
(info@gillmacmillan.ie)

Here I am

Challenging perceptions of Down syndrome in Ireland

Introduction

During the two years that I have been working on this project, I have been able to identify a common experience: many parents have told me about the initial surprise – sometimes shock – of finding out that their baby had Down syndrome, yet after a period of adjustment (and often times, despite dealing with severe medical issues) they tell me that their child has brought much joy and happiness into their lives. All the parents are convinced that their child has quite simply enhanced their lives, in spite of the challenges that accompany life with a child who has this condition.

I hope that as you look at this book, you will also enjoy reading the statements from the parents, because they have so much to say about their children, and that you can sense a great deal of hope and positivity in them. I have tried to capture the unique personality of each child in the photographs I took, and doing so was a lot of fun. It was also a great privilege to be able to spend time with them and their remarkable families.

I believe that society should re-evaluate its views on having a child with Down syndrome; that society should open its arms and embrace these children, as having much to teach us, and much warmth and love to offer us. I am reminded of a portion in Scriptures that says that truly "we are fearfully and wonderfully made". I have certainly discovered this as I met these wonderful individuals in the process of making this book: each one is a unique individual with his or her own gifts, talents, abilities and personality.

I would like to thank a few people who have helped me immensely to see this project through:

- my family who have been such a great support during the many hours of compiling this book.
- the people at Down Syndrome Ireland, and the various branches of DSI across the country, who have helped to set up all the photo shoots.
- our design team at Anú Design, who have been just fantastic.
- the logistical expertise of our distributors at Gill & Macmillan
- our printers at Dargan Press who have helped to make the book become reality.
- I also want to thank Vanessa for all her work and input.
- I also would like to thank Brendan for his encouragement and expertise.
- the parents who allowed me the privilege of photographing their children

But most of all, I would like to thank all the children who came to the photo shoots, for teaching me how wonderful and unique they truly are.

Dan Murphy
dtmurphy@eircom.net
www.dtmurphy.wix.com/danmurphyartist

Foreword

I realised very quickly when my daughter was born with Down syndrome that there was nothing wrong with her, it was the world that needed to change. Having a child with DS brings out different things in different people. Some people are really good at practical things like negotiating with state beaurocracies and raising money, while other people are more geared towards the epic sweep, towards changing the world.

When Dan came to me with this extraordinary project, I realised very quickly that while Dan is a practical man, a doer, in his heart he is one of those people who tolerates detail, but is really more interested in the broad sweep, the big picture. Dan does not want to fix people with DS, he wants to fix the rest of us. Because Dan knows that the biggest problem people with DS have is not DS; their real problem is the rest of us, how we look at them, how we condescend to them, how we see the signs, the mark, before we see the person. We put limits on them before we even know them. All too often it is not their DS that condemns them to a life set apart, it is how we see them that can set them apart.

So Dan set out to look without prejudice, as only a camera can. His lens removes all the additional layers and attitudes from the picture and just shows people in their beauty and their truth. And Dan's idea, I guess, is that everyone will take a second look, a real look, and not just see DS. Dan is in a great tradition here of challenging conventional notions of beauty, of making us look differently at something we see under our noses every day.

And, have no doubt, this is a challenging project. It will challenge those who usually look away. Or those who stare. It will challenge them to gaze instead. Indeed it will allow them to gaze in a way they might not feel they can in real life. It will challenge those who just glance and make simple assumptions to look properly and see individual children in all the glorious complexity that every child contains. On a very basic level, Dan is making the individual faces in this book, faces that can tend to be invisible to some people, visible.

And the most wonderful thing of all is that Dan's passion did not come from having a child with Down syndrome. Dan is not in the club, but he chose, in a sense, to join the club. And I'm sure the club welcomes him.

Brendan O'Connor

Amber, age 5

When Amber was born, we worried about her walking, talking, toileting and more, but she has taught us to be patient and take one day at a time. Amber has grown into a happy, friendly, active, musical, playful and determined girl who has her own personality and is well loved. She loves playing and having fun with her little sister (Jade), and enjoys going to school and meeting her friends and cousins. She loves her life and shows us what's really important.

Emma, age 3

From the moment that Emma was born, we made a promise to her that we would do everything it takes to insure that she has a fruitful and fulfilling life.

For her first three years, Emma was put through the mill with doctors and the system she was born into, but she came through like a rainbow breaking through a cloud. Emma is independent, resilient and she meets every day with a smile. She has reached and exceeded all her milestones and will continue to do so.

She continues to amaze everybody who knows her. Yes, Emma has Down syndrome and to those who don't know her, this matters; but to those of us who know her and love her, she is just Emma.

Matthew, age 4

Matthew never gives up. Against all the odds, he has made it. He is a warrior.

Millie, age 5 and her brother Camryn, age 4

Camryn was once asked the question, 'What do you see when you look at Millie?'
Camryn answered, 'She is my beautiful sister'.

Orla, age 1½

As big brother Niall says – the only thing wrong with Orla is that "she pulls my hair".
Orla is a pure little dote and we can't imagine her any other way.

Ben, age 2

Ben is a smiley, cuddly boy, but not because he has Down syndrome. He is who he is, not an angel or a gift from God, or anything other than a little boy who loves chocolate biscuits, sloppy kisses, singing and admiring himself in the mirror. He teaches us all patience as he blazes his own path and develops at his own rate. Milestone charts are seriously over-rated.

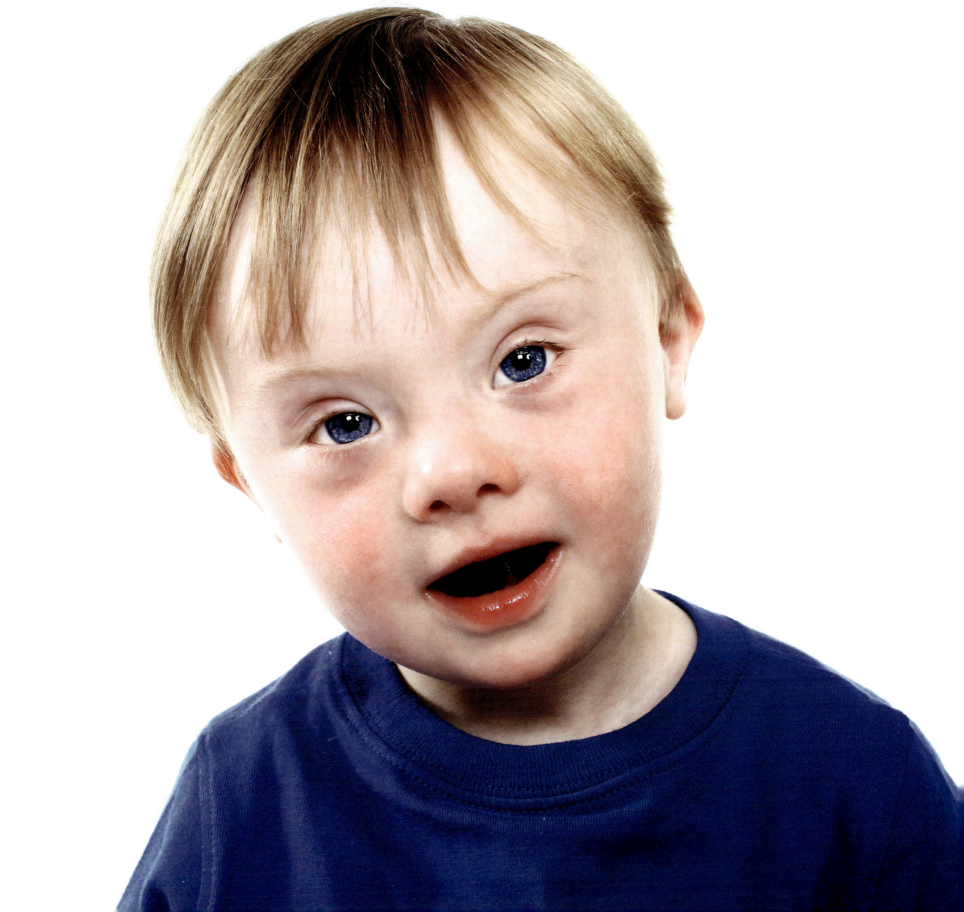

Rosa, age 3

Rosa is Rosa. Down syndrome is just an additional dimension to her wonderful person. While she shares some characteristics with other children who have Down syndrome, most of her characteristics, her personality, her talents, her interests are similar to those of her siblings. She is not one of 'them' – whoever 'they' are! She is one of us – the O'Connell family – and we are so lucky she is ours.

Tara, age 3

Tara is an amazing little girl and we love her to the moon and back.

Oisin, age 6

Oisin has an infectious laugh. He has a zest for life and loves living it.

Oisin is one of our four children. Oisin – with our other three children – is OUR FAMILY!

Aaron, age 6 with his sisters Megan and Caitlin

Our three special children: they are our world, they are funny, loving, mischievous, caring, naughty and nice. They love, fight and support each other. They also teach and learn from one another constantly – your typical family. They amaze us every day.

Megan, 8, loves reading, animals, GAA and drama. Megan loves to take part no matter what the event is. She is a very funny, thoughtful and kind young girl. She helps her brother and sister with their homework and comforts them when they are scared. Megan has a big heart and is a great big sister.

Aaron, 6, loves music, reading, drama and playing the drums. Aaron is a very sociable and kind boy, who loves to chat, he is full of questions and has a love of language. He adores his two sisters and he looks out for them both. He loves playing chasing and hiding games with them. He is a hard worker and is quite competitive. He loves to help out around the house. Aaron's smile and sense of humour light up every occasion.

Caitlin, 4, loves to sing, colour, drama and GAA. Caitlin is Aaron's teacher, minder, guide and best friend. She encourages him all the time. She is patient and kind and loves helping her brother and sister. Caitlin has a very infectious laugh and a beautiful smile. And if you are lucky enough to get a hug from Caitlin, treasure it, as it comes from the heart and they are not given lightly.

Leah, age 8

Leah is the light of our lives and we love her dearly. We are so proud of all she has achieved and we are honoured to be her parents.

Finn, age 3

Finn is similar to his older brother and sister in so many ways. He likes playing ball, swimming, wrestling on the floor, listening to nursery rhymes, getting into mischief, and eating sausages and cake... but he is also different in so many ways. These differences make Finn who he is: a happy, smiling, inquisitive and much loved son, brother, grandson, godson, nephew, neighbour, future teammate, colleague and friend. We love you lots Finn xx

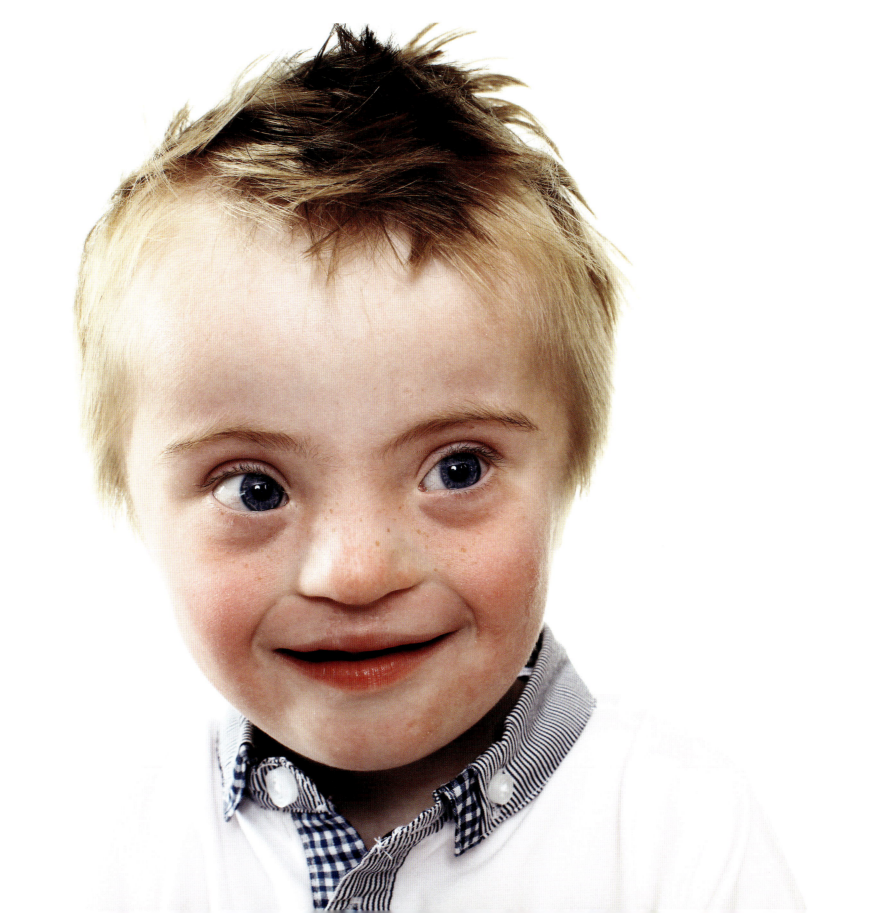

Aidan, age 21 months

We love Aidan's smile and hearty laugh. We also love how he warms our hearts so much.

Tara, age 7

The best thing about Tara is... everything.

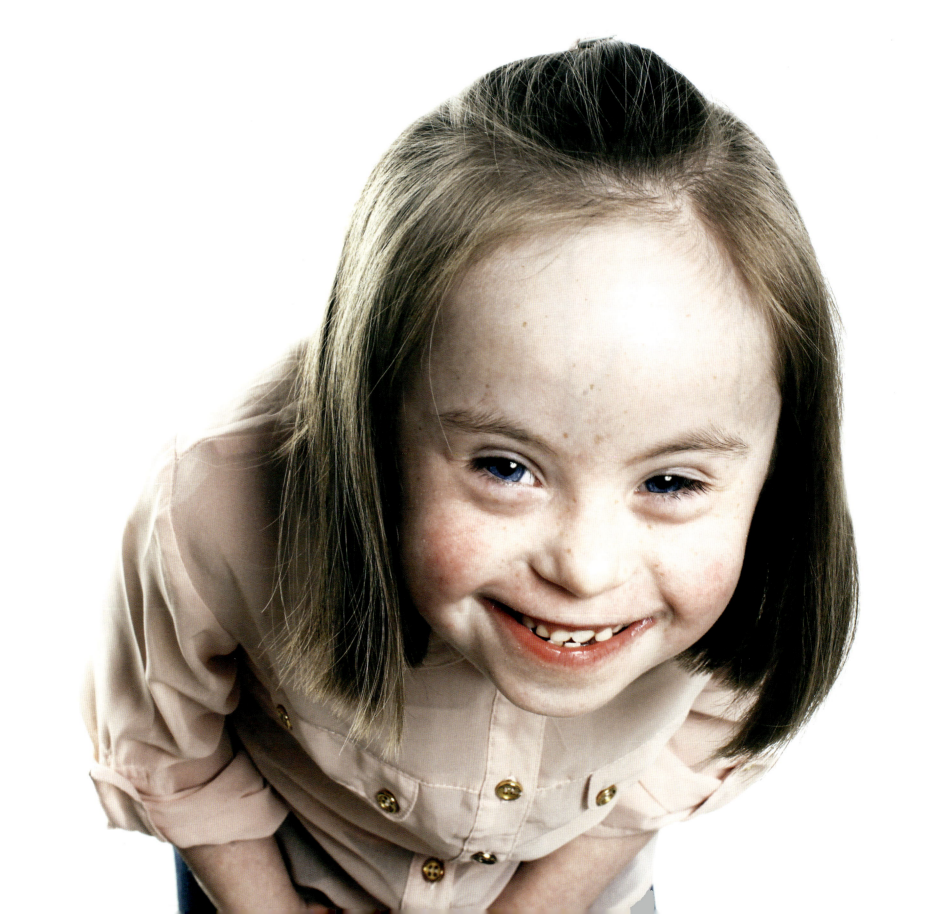

Katie, age 8

Katie is like every other 8 year old – she loves going to school, seeing her friends and being involved! Many a hill we have climbed together but we always come out on top, side by side. Katie's future is bright; she has a loving family behind her and with her bubbly, happy attitude to life, she will go far. She is an independent little girl with great determination.

Dara, age 2½

Having Dara has opened up a dimension in our lives and in our hearts that would otherwise have remained closed to us. We are learning more from him than he could ever learn from us. He is one of the three lights of our lives and we are truly grateful to call him ours.

Jason, age 8

Even when you think your whole world is collapsing, it just takes a smile
or a look from Jason to lift you.

Saoirse, age 9

This is our little Saoirse. She is 9 and was born a few weeks early arriving on her older sister's birthday – much to everyone's surprise. Saoirse was very sick in the early days and spent a lot of time in Crumlin. When she was 3 months old she had open-heart surgery and despite the odds, all went extremely well. Looking back now, it was her fighting spirit and determination – even as a small baby – that pulled her through. This same fighting spirit and determination is the backbone of Saoirse's personality now. She loves to be the centre of attention, loves performing, singing and dancing; a real character. She loves swimming and running, and has just won her first gold medal in the Munster Special Olympics. Her other great love would be animals, and she is very close to her dog. They have great chats. As it stands, Saoirse is a jolly, chatty little tom-boy, who loves the outdoors and climbing with her younger brother. She loves going away for nights – anywhere will do – from hotels to caravan parks – she's not fussy. She attends a special school not too far from her home, and loves playing with her friends. As for the future, we don't look too far ahead – she certainly doesn't and so far she has surpassed all of our expectations.

Chloe, age 3

I love the twinkle in her eyes.

Ben, age 2½

He loves balloons.

Cillian, age 11 months

Cillian has brought us so much love and hope. At birth he has had to fight through numerous medical problems but he has throughout it all managed to keep smiling.
He brings great joy and happiness to both our families.He is a lively and bubbly baby who is full of mischief. He brings a smile to our faces with his quirkiness.
In essense he is so cute so loving so huggable and just so special.

Natalie, age 5

Natalie is the bravest child that we have.

Apart from the families of Down syndrome children, the general public doesn't give children with Down syndrome credit for the daily battles they have with activities that we all take for granted. This makes them the strongest people in society but yet they are treated as if they have nothing to give.

We all need to wake up and open our eyes...

Daniel, age 6

I like having fun and laughing – My best trick is to cover my face with my hands and groan and dramatically say "Oh no", then peek through my fingers and smile – fooled ya!. I do love to make time for bedtime stories with my Mum and Dad; my favourites at the moment are Peter Rabbit and Peter Pan. I love being me!

Anthony, age 6

Anthony is fun loving, even though he is only six, he truly loves life and he is loved by everyone around him. We simply could not imagine life without him.

Odhran, age 2 and his sister Aoibheann, age 3

There is 16 months between the two of them, they are very close.

He loves to copy his big sister every day.

Laila, age 2½

The saying goes that mothers support their children, but our little girl supports us all.
She lifts me up every day and makes me realise small things in life don't matter.
Life without our little girl would feel incomplete.

Laila's Mom

My little sister was a gift from God; the most precious gift anybody could receive.
Laila, to me, is the definition of unconditional love.

Laila's sister

Lily, age 4

Since the day our baby Lily was born she has changed our lives in unexplainable ways. Lily has the biggest, bluest eyes in the world, which are so full of love and happiness. Our love for Lily is a special kind of love. Although Lily hasn't found words yet, she shows her love for us with her big hugs and special kisses, which are like no other.

Lily is only four but likes to be stylish and cool, like her older sisters, who are her idols, and of course she loves to make them laugh! Lily is like no other little girl in the world and she continues to surprise us everyday with her unconditional love. We know that nothing will ever stop our special princess. Everyday we look forward to an exciting future with Lily, and can't wait to see what else she has in store for us. Our biggest hope for Lily for the future is that she will always be happy.

Leon, age 10

He has a great sense of humour. He is a gifted mimic, and full of empathy for all and sundry.

Thomas, age 3

Thomas is our sunshine, he is full of fun, he loves people.

Sophie, age 2½

Sophie lights up my world.

Sadhbh, age 1

Beautiful, happy, smiley, resilient, cuddly, funny, strong-willed, curious,
brave, determined and vocal – Sadhbh is all of these plus many more,
but most of all, she is quite simply herself. She is our little girl,
who we are extremely proud of and love so much.

Kyle, age 5

Kyle is a typical fun loving boy who loves to play and entertain. His energy is boundless.
He has a wonderful sense of humour and finds fun and joy in everyday life.

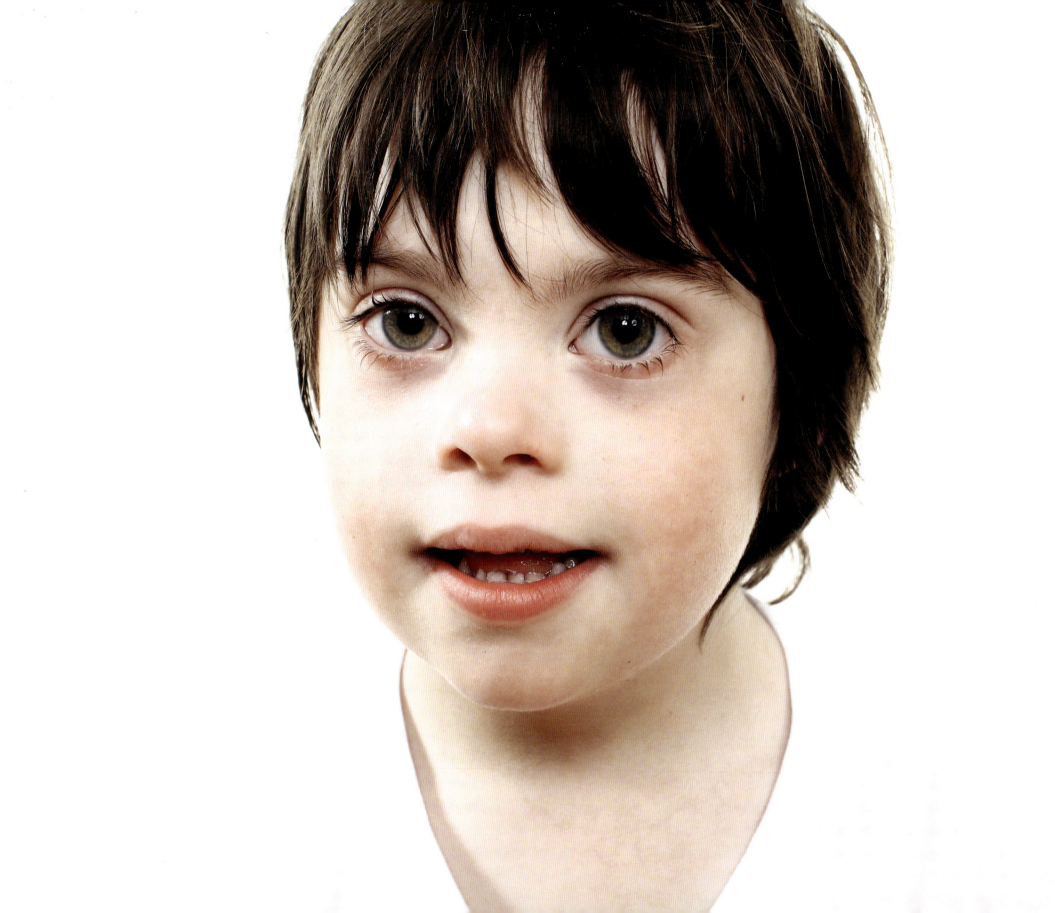

Rafael, age 2

My son inspires me every day with his perseverance.
At times it seems difficult, but he always succeeds.

Gráinne, age 5

Grainne loves being with her older siblings. She is a really little 'toughy'.
She and her pet dog, rule the roost!!

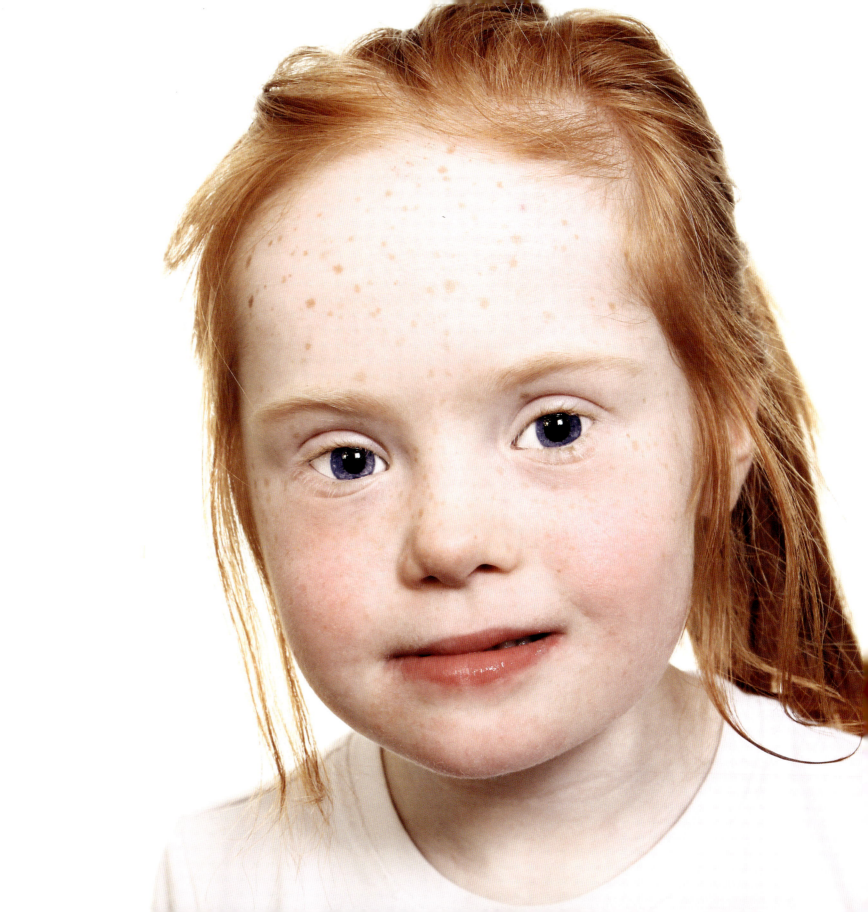

Alice, age 6

Alice has been our greatest joy (and our greatest sorrow, health-wise!) but we are actually the luckiest Mum and Dad in the world!

Harry, age 8

Harry isn't restricted by what other people think, and he lives every experience to the full, in his own unique way.

Shane, age 9 and his sister Nancy

Shane has grown into a confident and self-assured boy. He adores reading, watching Jamie Oliver cooking programs and playing with his sister Nancy (most of the time!).

James, age 11

James loves Laurel and Hardy movies!

Maddix, age 14 months

Maddix is a ray of sunshine and the apple of our eyes. She is confident and has a lovely sense of humour. Her personality and smile will melt your heart. She is beautiful inside and out. We are so in love with her...

Sky, age 2½

"We never know how high we are, till we are called to rise; and then, if we are true to plan, our statures touch the sky." – Emily Dickinson

Sky Legend Moran

Sky is the youngest of six children and the heart of our family. He was born with beautiful blue eyes, orangey-red hair, chubby cheeks, long skinny legs, a strong grip, a calm and determined disposition, and a melt-your-heart smile. At 2½ years old, he still has all of that – and is clever, funny, and full of joy too!

What's with that name?

When we were expecting Sky, our 4 year old son said he'd like to name the baby Sky because 'It's the most beautiful thing I can think of'. We went with that! How could we not? When Sky was about a week old, he came to the hospital to meet his baby brother for the first time and as soon as he walked into Sky's hospital room, despite all the machines and tubes coming out of this tiny baby, his face lit up with a smile and the first thing he said was, 'see Mommy, I told you – he's beautiful!' So true – Sky IS beautiful in every way.

Because Daddy loves maps and Mommy loves stories, we said to Sky in his blessing, 'may you weave a beautiful story through life, guided on your path by the knowledge that your home is always within the heart of your family.'

Aoife, age 7

She is simply the best.

Amanda, age 2

Amanda is a beautiful child. She is always in good humour and happy. She is a pleasure to bring anywhere because she is always happy. Since Amanda arrived, she has taught us a lot. Amanda is proof that any problem can be overcome. We thank God that Amanda is in our lives

Timmy, age 5

What I love most about Timmy is his infectious belly laugh! When he laughs in public, people around us start smiling and laughing too.

Evan, age 4½

Evan has the most amazing smile and personality,
which seems to touch everybody he meets.

Sophie, age 3

Sophie is our own little ray of sunshine. She is a gentle, sensitive, funny, mischievous, typical three-year-old. She adores and torments her little sister in equal measures. She is brimming over with love for everyone and is always first in line to give a hug when it is needed

Of course, when she was born and we were told she had Down syndrome, we shed many tears. We were filled with fear for her future and ours. We had very little experience of Down syndrome and it was that ignorance that fanned the flames of our fears.

However, Sophie wouldn't let us give in to our fears. She smiled her way into everyone's hearts, and Down syndrome soon took a backseat to the pleasures of being her parents. She has overcome all her challenges in her own calm and determined little way, and we have realised that if she can face her challenges without fear then we can too. Our hope for her future is that she continues to be strong and determined, but mainly that she is happy in whatever she does. If the world can continue to grow in its acceptance and encouragement of people with Down syndrome then the future is very bright for Sophie.

Peter, age 4½

Peter is an integral part of our family. It was a rocky start, due to his health problems, but he has blossomed into a happy, healthy, active child who loves life and his family.

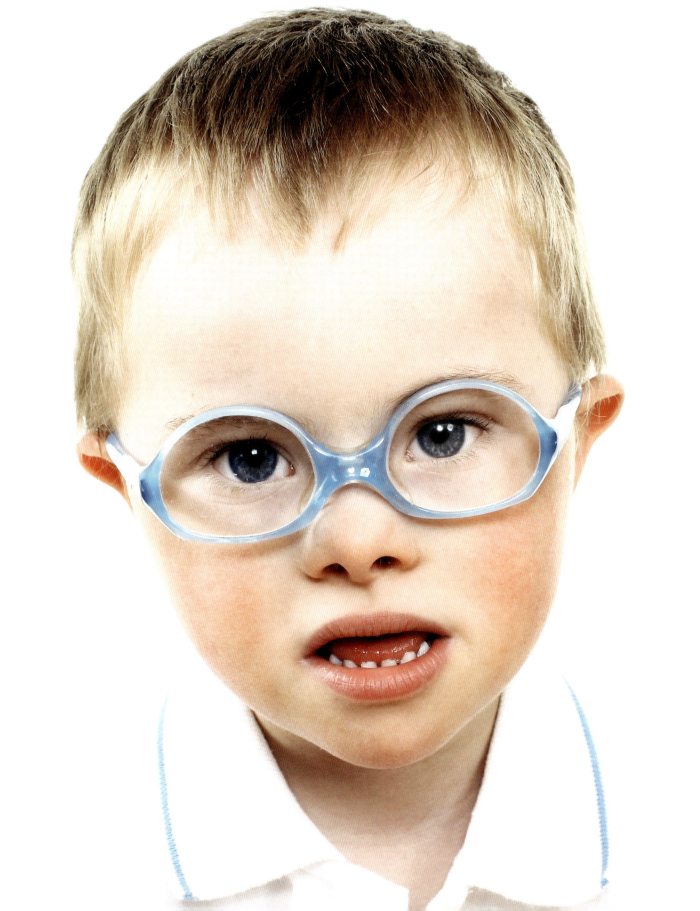

Amy, age 5

Amy is thoughtful, happy, cuddly and content, and she loves dancing.

James, age 11

We as a family would describe James as contagious, infectious and he opens our eyes in the most fantastic way every single day.

Moyo, age 10

Our lives wouldn't be the same without Moyo. There is never a dull moment with him around. We see God's goodness daily, manifested in every forward step that Moyo takes. We can all learn so much from our precious and special children.

Caitriona, age 4

What I love about my daughter is her sense of fun, adventure and sheer determination. Her perseverance to achieve things that come easier to others, is an example to me.

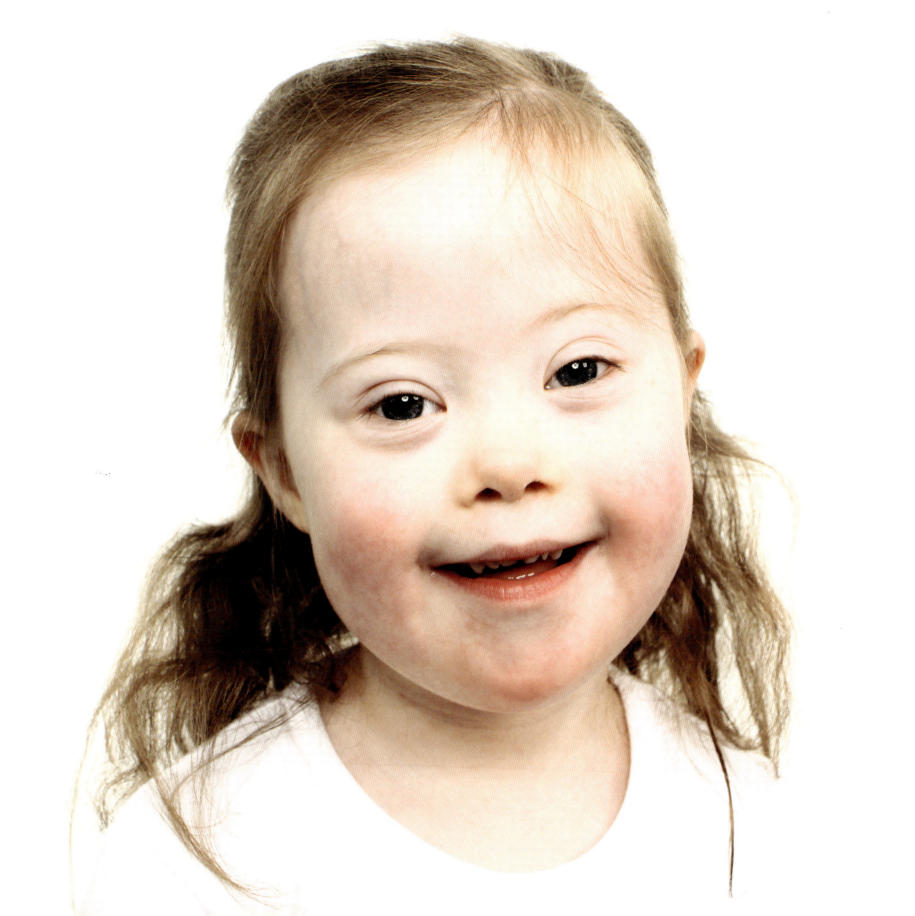

Katie, age 6

Katie is our little miracle girl who is charming, mischievous and has a cheeky smile. She is a brave warrior who never ceases to amaze us.

Oisin, age 3½

Oisin is a bright and beautiful boy with a big smile and a bigger heart. Being the youngest of five, he loves to be part of the fun and games, and his hearty laugh always brings a smile to our faces. Oisin's enthusiasm to meet people and discover the world around him has given us great hope for his future.

Joshua, age 10

Beautiful, caring, funny and clever.

Emma, age 5

Emma is the most enchanting kind and honestly-loving child. Emma has a will
and determination that will carry her to the greatest of heights and we, her family,
will hold her heart, and watch on with extraordinary pride.

Lily, age 4

Lily brightens up every day.

Jessica, age 22 months

We found out Jessica would have Down syndrome when I was 20 weeks pregnant. At first we were upset. As parents you don't want anything to be wrong with any of your children. Of course we thought how would we cope? What would her future hold? All the usual thoughts and fears. However, as Jessica's arrival drew near we had educated ourselves about Down syndrome and we were happy to have Jessica arrive into our lives.

We hope that whatever Jessica dreams of doing in the future will become a reality for her. We hope that just because she has Down syndrome, people see her for who she is as a person and not just her condition.

Dearbhla, age 3½

She gives us lots of hugs and kisses, and she loves music.

Fionn, age 10

Everything that is good to be seen in the world can be seen in his radiant smile.
Everything that brings happiness and healing can be felt in his warm, gentle hug.

Darragh, age 6 and Cian, age 5

Cian and Darragh are brothers and best friends. Some people think they are twins but Darragh is a year older. They both love running, climbing, wrestling, and eating chocolate and ice cream. Cian doesn't have Down syndrome but he doesn't really mind.

Alex, age 4

Alex is fun and always up to mischief. We hope Alex gets to do what he loves when he grows up, whatever that may be. At the present moment, it's dancing and "pow! pow!" but who knows what it will be in the future. Alex makes people laugh and – despite the popular belief that all kids with Down syndrome are so 'happy and placid' – he is extremely discerning about who he wants to amuse and connect with. That is what I love about my child.
I hope he never grows out of that.

Maeve, age 5

Our lives changed completely 5 years ago with the surprise arrival of Maeve.
We wouldn't change her for the world!

Andrew, age 7

Andrew meets and greets EVERYONE in his school every morning. His favourite mornings are when he arrives at the same time as the school bus and he gets to meet and greet everyone at the school gate with a smile, a wave, and a personal greeting! Nobody is ignored or left out.

Brian, age 5

We love Brian's constant love and affection for those he holds dear.
We love his limitless appetite for fun and mischief. We love his laughter,
his hugs and kisses, and his infectious good humour.

Rachel, age 3

Rachel has made our family. She makes us laugh and smile every single day.
She is the light of our lives.

Darragh, age 6

Darragh is very loyal to his loved ones. He would never let anyone down.
A great guy with a big heart.

James, age 5½

James is a happy, social, determined young boy. We love that he brings a vibrant energy
and joy to our family. He is like any other little boy of his age, except for one thing …
his smile shines that little bit brighter.

Rose, age 4

Rose is our little angel – unique in every way. She spreads love and happiness wherever she goes. We are blessed to have her in our lives.

Lara, age 12

Lara has a great sense of humour, she loves sports and all kinds of music.
She and her sister are best of friends.

Charlie, age 4

Charlie is a fun, loveable child and is loved by all who know him.

Eoin, age 5

Summary of our feelings the Day Eoin was born:

Emotional – So Scared, no idea of what lies ahead, what health issues Eoin may have, guilt, fear.

Overwhelmed – What Impact will DS have on Eoin, on our lives, on our other children?

Inadequte – Do we have the skills to deal with this diagnosis, to help Eoin achieve his full potential?

Nurture – Innate and unconditional love for Eoin, our baby, not a DS baby, just our baby.

Summary of our feelings 5 years later as Eoin starts Mainstream Primary School:

Excitement – Every day brings new achievements/challenges for both Eoin and us.

Over-awed – Our little man shows ability as opposed to disability in so many different ways and guises

Incensed – By the lack of awareness/attitudes of so many people in power who don't provide access to community supports that Eoin needs and deserves.

Nervous – Fearful for what the future holds but will continue to strive with Eoin for endless possibilities.

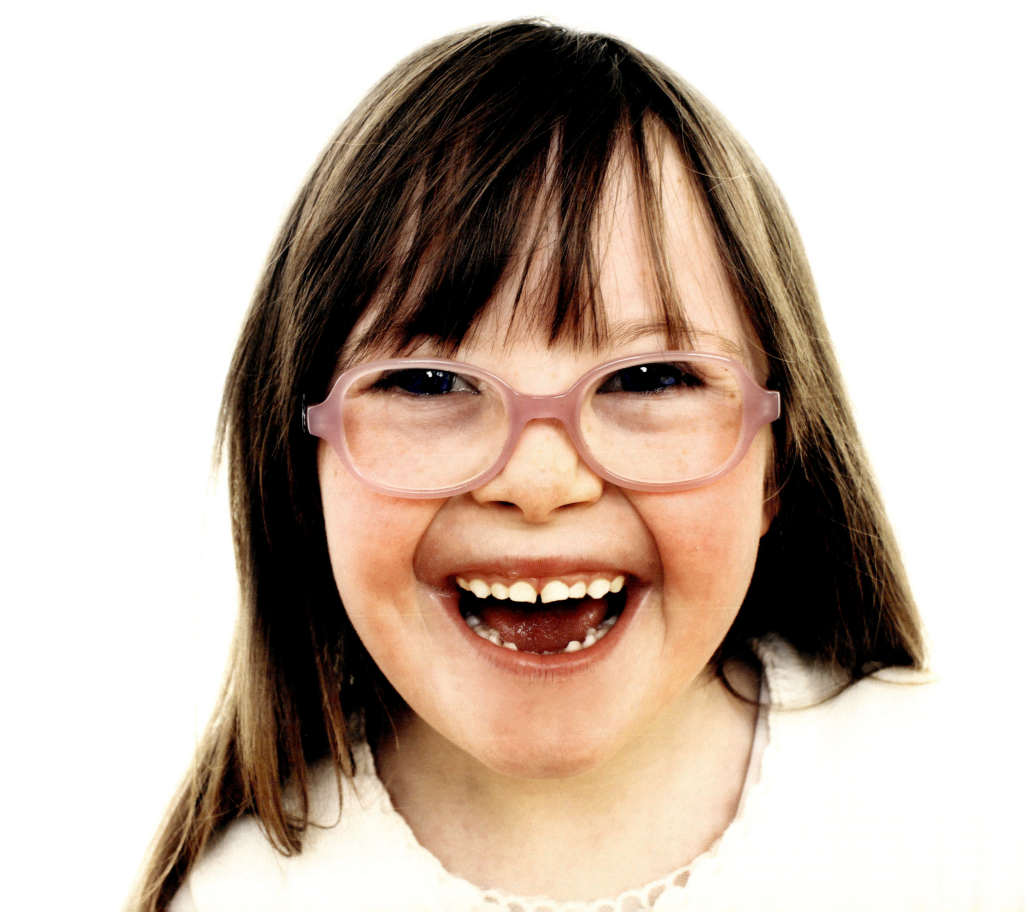

Maria, age 6

Maria is a very special girl. She has a beautiful smile and an endearing warm personality. She bravely fought leukaemia for two and a half years. She has shown strength of character and courage that astounded everybody around her. She has a mischievous personality and loves fun. Everybody that is around her has to get a hug. She is much loved. A precious gift is Maria.

Daniel, age 3

Daniel is a curious and lively boy who has brought endless joy into our lives.
He brightens up each and every day.

Liam, age 7

Liam is full of personality and energy. He loves to entertain people.

His current favourite is to sing 'Let It Go' and 'Do You Want to Build a Snowman?'

from the movie Frozen – both sung at the top of his lungs with all the actions.

He makes us laugh everyday!

Amy, age 2½

Amy is our love, our life, our everything. She would brighten up anyone's day. Amy is very independent and doesn't let anything slow her down. She is gorgeous and loving, and a very happy little girl. Amy brings us love and happiness and we are grateful every day, that she is a part of our family. We love her to bits.

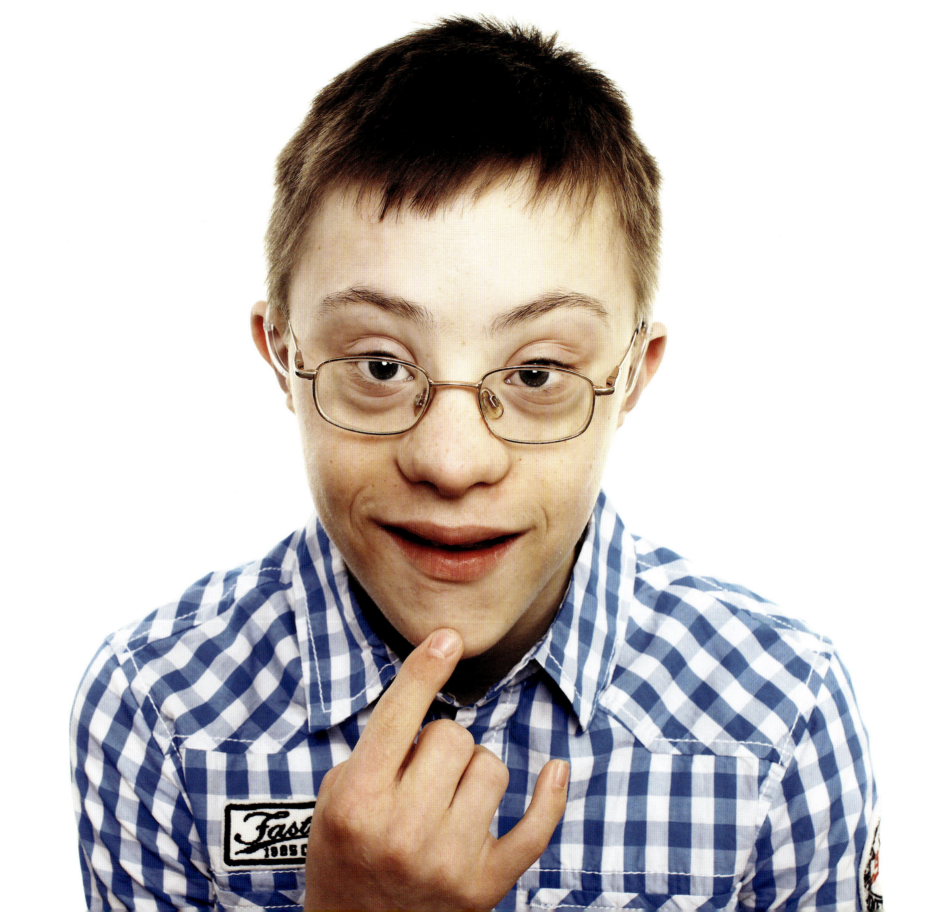

Daniel, age 12

Our loveable rogue.

Harry, age 4

Our Harry is like a beautiful rainbow in our black and white world.

Jamie, age 16 months

We love and appreciate everything about Jamie. He may have Down syndrome
but that is only one little thing about him, and probably the least important.
Jamie is a chilled-out dude who loves a good laugh and flirting with anybody he can.
Our life changed dramatically the day Jamie was born. Little did we know at the time
but it changed for the better.

Peppy, age 6

My name is Peppy. When I was younger I had a few problems with my heart and I also had to get my food through a tube in my nose. Then I got my heart fixed and I learnt to eat and drink by myself.

During the week I go to school and I love it. I talk using my hands; it's called Lámh, but what is totally cool is that my teacher has taught all my friends in the class how to use it!

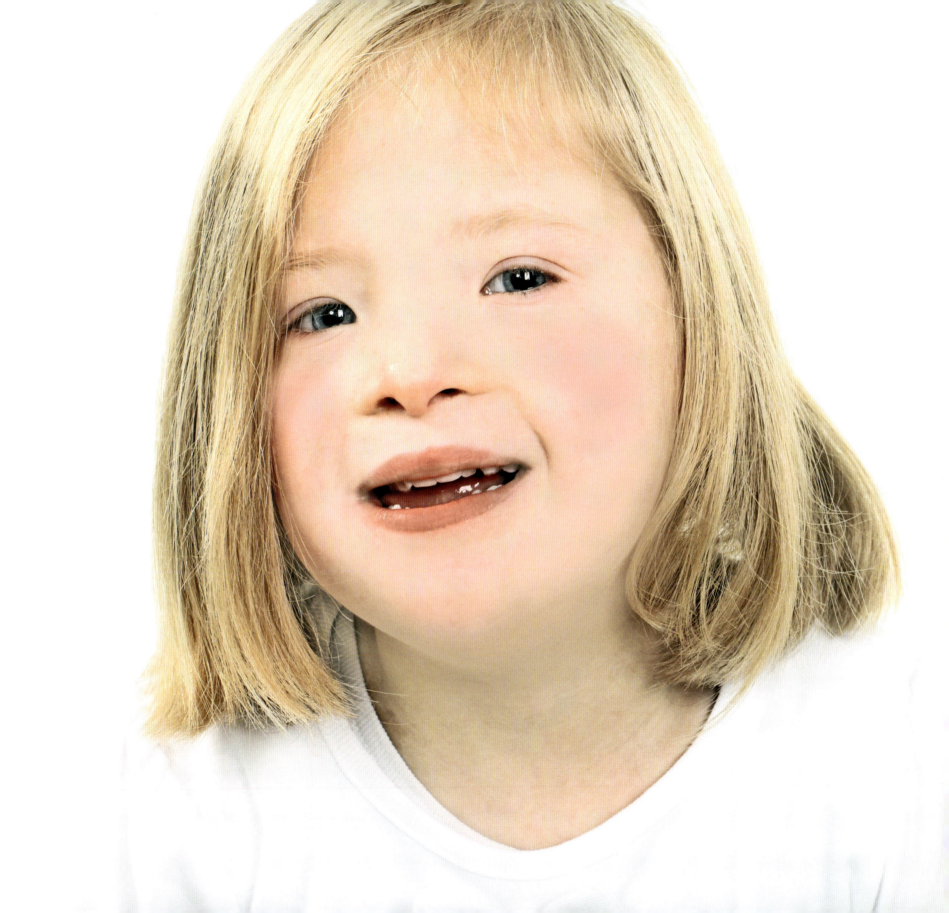

Joe, age 6

When Joe was born, he spent 4 months in the hospital before finally coming home.
Life with Joe is not always easy, but the good times far outweigh the difficult ones.
One of the most precious time of the day with Joe is when he is going to bed,
he hugs all of us and says "goodnight" and "I love you".

Joe loves life and everyone, and in turn, he is loved by all he meets.

Killian, age 11

Killian is the practical joker of our family. He is a great lad for helping out around the home. He loves movies. Killian also loves swimming. He is very affectionate, and absolutely adores his family.

Leah, age 8

Leah is 8 years old and has one sister and two brothers. Leah is the third in our family. She is in first class in main stream school and enjoys it very much. Her favourite subject is reading. Her hobbies include horse riding, swimming, irish dancing and speech and drama. She has a fantastic personality and always full of fun and laughter.

Joe, age 4

Joe has opened many doors of friendship, honesty and openness.
He makes great connections with people.

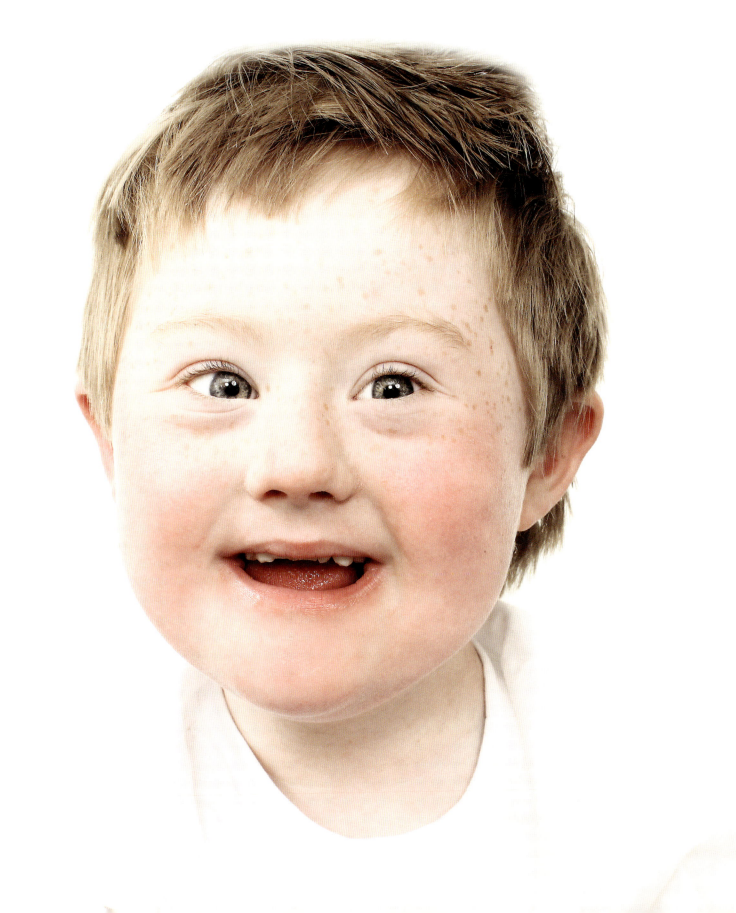

Dylan, age 6½

Dylan is a little man with a big heart.

Christopher, age 6

Christopher lives in the moment, and I love the enthusiasm he brings into our lives.

Lucy, age 4

Lucy's Gift to Me – As a parent of a child with Down syndrome I have been taught
to see the person not the disability and I am so thankful every day for that gift.
I think I'm one of the lucky ones in life. I have been given a glimpse of what
'Heaven' is about ... a place where you see past the outer shell, to the beauty
of a person's spirit and soul. Thank you Lucy.

Keane, age 22 months

Our little boy has brought out such joy and happiness that we never ever
thought we would feel, holding him the night he was born. It felt like the worst
night ever. Everyone else said that we were given a gift and that we were so lucky.
I can't say that we agreed at the time but looking back now, I do feel that we
are the luckiest parents on the planet.

Liam, age 1

"Let your smile change the world but don't let the world change your smile."

Sarah, age 2

Sarah is a happy little girl.

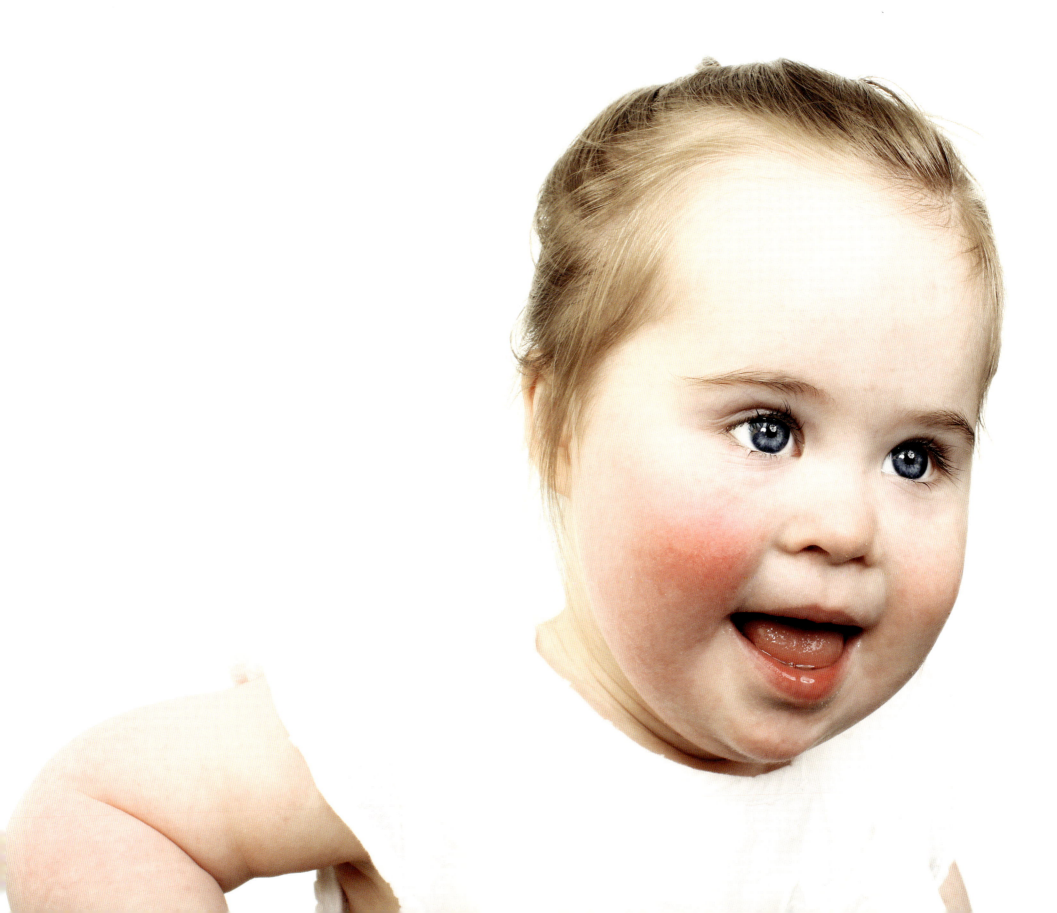

Noah, age 6

Noah is our eldest child and the heartbeat of our family. He is funny, smart and mischievous. He loves life, bread and chips. Noah never complains about the extra challenges and work he faces at home and school, and he continues to dispel his perceived limitations. As Noah grows, so does our understanding of his abilities and what he can strive to achieve in life.

In memory of

Sarah Dillon

2nd July 2004 – 12th April 2014

Our beautiful Sarah was full of love and happiness.
She touched the hearts of everyone who met her.
Her life was short, but Sarah filled every minute of it.

National Leadership Local Support

Down Syndrome Ireland is a family led organisation that places the person with Down syndrome at the centre of everything that we do. Their diverse needs, as well as the needs of their families, are our primary focus and concern.

On behalf of, and together with every unique individual with Down syndrome in Ireland, we are committed to working towards an Irish society where people with Down syndrome are respected and accepted as valued members of our society.

The services we provide to people with Down syndrome, young and old, and their families continue to evolve and develop, to keep up with the modern landscape and all the new challenges that this brings. Services include a home teacher programme; speech and language therapy; early developmental programmes; occupational therapy; Latch On, an innovate and very successful adult literacy programme; social skills etc.

Many of our programmes and activities are viewed as best in class, both nationally and internationally. This ethos of quality and progress we strive to uphold, to deliver the best possible results for our members and their individual needs.

The volunteering efforts and ethos of our members has been core to the success and development of our organisation since its inception in 1971. We have 26 very individual and active branches around the country which are run by parents and relatives who volunteer their time and work tirelessly to provide vital services for our members at a local level. The organisation is supported by our national office in Dublin, with a team of extremely dedicated and experienced professionals.

On behalf of everyone in Down Syndrome Ireland we would like to take this opportunity to thank you for your support.

Please do not hesitate to contact us at the address below if you would like any further information.

Down Syndrome Ireland, Citylink Business Park, Old Naas Road, Dublin 12.
Tel: 01 426 6500   Low-call number: 1 890 374 374   email: info@downsyndrome.ie